Bread

Honor Head

QED Publishing

Copyright © QED Publishing 2006

First published in the UK in 2006 by
QED Publishing
A Quarto Group company
226 City Road
London EC1V 2TT
www.qed-publishing.co.uk

A Catalogue record for this book is available from the British Library.

ISBN 1 84538 373 7

Written by Honor Head
Designed by Danny Pyne
Edited by Hannah Ray and Barbara Bourassa
Consultancy by Roy Balam and Sarah Schenker of the British Nutrition Foundation
Photographer Michael Wicks
Illustrations by Bill Greenhead

Publisher Steve Evans
Art Director Zeta Davies
Editorial Director Jean Coppendale

Printed and bound in China

Picture credits
Key: t = top, b = bottom, c = centre, l = left, r = right, FC = front cover
Alamy/Danita Delimont 23cr; **Corbis**/Jacqui Hurst br/ Hanan Isachar 23tl/ Earl
& Nazima Kowall 26tr/ Becky Lulgart-Stayner 26cl/ PhotoCuisine 27cl/ Nobert Schaefer
FC/ TH-Foto/Zefa 23bl; **Dorling Kindersley**/25tr/ 27tr; **Getty images**/Stockfood Creative
Dorota & Bogdan Blaly 27br/ StockFood Creative Louise Lister 24bl.

Before undertaking any activity which involves eating or the preparation of food,
always check whether the children in your care have any food allergies. In a classroom
situation, prior written permission from parents may be required.

Website information is correct at time of going to press. However, the publishers
cannot accept liability for any information or links found on third-party websites.

Words in **bold** can be found in the glossary on page 30.

Contents

It's about balance!

Eating a balanced diet is really important for helping our bodies to grow strong and healthy. A balanced diet means eating the right mix of different types of food, but what should we eat to make sure our diet is balanced?

Weblink

Some countries, such as the USA and Australia, use a food pyramid instead of a plate to help explain how to eat a healthy, balanced diet. To find out more, visit www.mypyramid.gov/kids

Mix it up

A balanced diet is important because no one food can provide everything your body needs to stay healthy and to work properly. To give your body what it needs, you need to eat a mix of different types of foods.

Food in five

All food can be put into one of five main groups:

fruit and vegetables
(for example, apples, broccoli, green beans and fruit juice)

Some foods are better for us than others, which means our bodies need more food from some groups than from others. The plate diagram shows how much of your diet should be made up of food from each group.

bread, other cereals and potatoes
(such as bread, breakfast cereals and pasta)

milk and dairy foods
(includes things such as milk, cheese and yoghurt)

meat, fish and alternatives
(such as pork, beef, chicken, tuna and tofu)

foods that contain fats and sugars
(for example, butter, mayonnaise, sweets and jam)

Top Tip!

If you need help remembering how to eat a balanced diet, think of it this way: a third of what you eat should be fruit and vegetables; a third should be bread, other cereals and potatoes; and the final third should be made up of the other food groups (meat and fish, dairy foods and foods that contain fat or sugar). Even simpler? Eat more food from the large sections, and less from the small sections. It's easy!

Why eat bread?

This book is all about bread, from the bread, other cereals and potatoes food group. Bread comes in many different shapes, colours and flavours. It is an essential part of our daily diet and provides **carbohydrate**, **fibre**, **vitamins** and **minerals**. Try to eat some bread every day.

Science bit!

Bread is made from **grains**, such as wheat. These grains contain fibre, which is not digested by the body. Instead, the fibre passes through the body, helping to keep us healthy.

Kinds of carbs

Carbohydrates are the main source of energy in the diet. We get carbohydrates from bread, pasta, potatoes, rice and cereals. Foods such as cakes, biscuits and sweets also provide carbohydrates, but as a type of sugar. We should try to eat less of these foods and more bread, cereals and potatoes for a healthy, balanced diet.

Bite size

Bread is made of flour and water, with added salt for taste and **yeast** to make it rise.

Brown vs. white

Okay, so we know that bread is good for you, but some bread is better than others. The good part is all in the bran, which is part of the wheat grain. In white bread, which has been refined, bran and some of the **nutrients** are lost. In wholegrain bread, which is brown, the bran and all the other good stuff is left in. For a healthy and balanced diet, a variety of different types of bread is best.

Ready, bready, go!

There are loads of different types of bread. Here are just a few **types** of bread that you can see in most shops and supermarkets:

Soda bread

Naan bread

Pitta bread

White sliced

Fruit loaf

Bagels

French stick

Lunch choice

A sandwich is an ideal lunchbox choice. It's easy to make and easy to eat, but how can you make your sandwiches the bread winners?

Gold-star sandwiches

If you really don't like brown bread, why not try a multicoloured double-decker? Have a slice of wholegrain white bread on the top and bottom, and a slice of brown in the middle. Alternatively, why not try some different breads that are just as good for you and tops for taste?

Cheese salad sandwich

Bottle of water

Wholegrain white top and bottom

Banana

Bagel

Brown roll

Rye bread

Weblink
For some great ideas for tasty sandwich fillings visit www.easy-kids-recipes.com/easy-lunch-recipes.html

8

Gross!

You can put nearly anything in a sandwich but some things, such as tomatoes, can make the bread soggy by lunchtime and then it can fall through your fingers and drip down your front! For a drip-free sandwich, keep the tomato slices separate and slip them in just before you eat the sandwich.

Slice of brown in the middle

Cheese and salad filling

Bite size

Spread butter thinly onto bread, or choose olive or sunflower spread. If your sandwich filling is sticky, you don't need butter at all.

SUPER
SANDWICH FILLINGS

Here are some great ideas for tasty and nutritious sandwiches:

- Tuna and cucumber
- Sliced egg with cress
- Chicken salad
- Ham and coleslaw
- **Houmous** with lettuce
- Sliced sausage with tomato

How bread is made (1)

Bread is made from flour. Before we can make bread, the flour has to be **processed**.

From field to flour

Wheat is a grain that grows in fields.

When the wheat is ripe, it is harvested. This means it is cut and made into bundles.

These bundles, or sheaves, are taken by lorry to a factory where the wheat is milled into flour.

Changing the wheat into flour is called the milling process.

The milling process

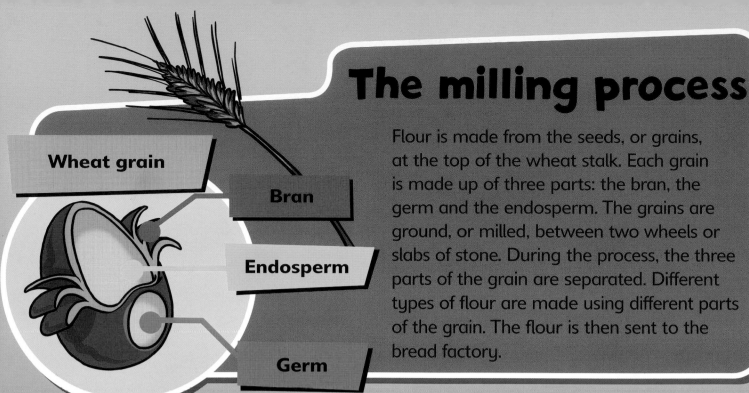

Wheat grain

Bran

Endosperm

Germ

Flour is made from the seeds, or grains, at the top of the wheat stalk. Each grain is made up of three parts: the bran, the germ and the endosperm. The grains are ground, or milled, between two wheels or slabs of stone. During the process, the three parts of the grain are separated. Different types of flour are made using different parts of the grain. The flour is then sent to the bread factory.

Flour power

Bread can be made from many different types of flour. Here's a quick round-up to keep you ahead of bread:

White bread
Made from flour that contains only the middle of the grain, the endosperm.

Wholegrain bread
This is bread made with white flour but with added **wholegrains** to increase the amount of fibre.

Brown bread
Made from flour which includes the endosperm and a small amount of the bran.

Other breads

You might also have tried wholemeal bread. This is bread made with flour that uses all of the wheat grain. And have you heard of wheatgerm bread? This is made from brown or white flour but has some of the germ of the grain added for extra flavour. There are heaps of other types of bread, made from different flours. Why not try some and see which is your favourite?

How bread is made (2)

So we've got the flour, now onto the bread factory...

Weblink

Fancy making some bread? Visit www.nutrition.org.uk and click on 'Education', 'Cook club', 'Primary school recipes' and 'Bread' for a simple recipe.

1

The flour is poured into huge silos (containers). Other ingredients, such as yeast, salt and vitamins, are then added. The flour is then mixed with water and **kneaded** to make the first stage of the bread **dough**.

Check out the size of those silos!

2

The dough is cut and shaped, ready to drop into bread tins.

Into the tins – hope they don't miss!

12

3

The conveyor belt takes the tins to a **proving** area, where the bread swells up in size. The bread tins then pass through a hot oven where the bread is baked.

4

The baked loaves are sucked out of the tins and pass through a machine which cools them. They are then checked for quality.

Mmm, freshly baked bread smells great!

5

Right – I'm off for a sarnie!

Finally, the loaves are sliced, wrapped and loaded onto lorries for delivery to the shops and supermarkets.

Next stage... your tum!

Lunch choice

Pizza slice

The base of a pizza is made from dough, similar to that used to make bread. A tasty slice of pizza makes a delicious change from a sandwich and is easy to eat with your fingers – but make sure you've washed your hands first!

Pizza perfect

A cheese and tomato pizza is a great balanced meal. A thick base provides plenty of carbohydrate. The tomato topping is a rich source of vitamin A, and sprinkling a little cheese on top provides calcium. Adding slices of chicken or ham will give you **protein**, and vegetable toppings or a side salad will count towards your recommended five **portions** of fruit and vegetables a day. To make your pizza even more perfect, try a brown flour version – it's just as tasty.

Fruit juice

Cheese and tomato pizza slices

Wholemeal pizza base

Get kneading

Some shop-bought pizzas contain high levels of salt and fat, so check the label to see exactly what you're getting. Better still, make your own pizza base and add mix 'n' match toppings. Here are some ideas:

Tuna

Green pepper

Cheese

Tomatoes

Sweetcorn

Onion

Ham

Asparagus

Mushrooms

Tub of salad

Try it!

Keep fried dough, such as doughnuts, as a treat – too many and you might turn into a dough person!

?

Q. When is a pizza not a pizza?
A. When it's a pudding!

Some restaurants are experimenting with sweet toppings for dessert pizzas, such as ice cream, peaches, nuts, strawberries and apple slices. Yum!

Cake, anyone?

Cakes and biscuits can be made from lots of different ingredients but, like bread, they are made from a base of flour.

Weblink
Have fun making delicious snacks to go in your lunchbox. Visit www.flourandgrain.com/recipes/recipes5.asp for an easy-to-follow recipe for tasty oat and fruit bars.

Sugar showdown

Too much sugar is the baddie of any healthy diet. However, it comes in lots of different forms and some sugar is needed as part of a balanced diet. Foods such as fruit contain natural sugars, which is why they taste sweet. Cakes, chocolate and fizzy drinks have sugar added. This is processed sugar made from sugar cane and sugar beet. Too much of this type of sugar can be bad for you.

Can I have my cake and eat it?

A large slice of chocolate fudge cake with extra cream is delicious as an occasional treat, but for an everyday snack try some healthy choices – they needn't be boring! Fruit cake, carrot cake, gingerbread, small currant buns and low-fat muffins are all tasty treats.

Biscuit bar

For a quick and easy snack, you can't beat a biscuit. Stick to dried fruit and **muesli** bars and make the odd chocolate bar a treat.

Fruit juice

Sandwiches

Muffin

Apple

Well balanced

If you are feeling really hungry at lunchtime, try not to fill up on sweet things. Eat a sandwich or a roll first, have a drink of juice or water and then, if you're still hungry, have a small slice of cake, a biscuit or a low-fat muffin. Sweet stuff should be a once-a-day treat, rather than a major part of your diet. Remember, keep it balanced!

Lunch choice

Pitta fingers with dips

This fun lunch is great for sharing with friends or just enjoying all by yourself.

Brown pitta bread cut into fingers

Houmous

Pick a pitta pocket

Pitta is a traditional bread made in Greece and Turkey. It is a flat bread and can be made with white or brown flour. Pittas are used as pockets for cooked lamb slices and salad to make a type of kebab. You can put any kind of filling in a pitta pocket, just like a sandwich.

Try it!

Spread a pitta bread with your favourite spread. Once you have sliced it, your pitta dippers will have a fab filling!

Dip in

Use pitta fingers, made from sliced pitta breads, to scoop up some delicious dips. Try these:

Garlic dip (made from yoghurt and garlic)

Fresh tzatziki (made from yoghurt and cucumber)

Guacamole (made from avocado)

Bottle of water

Fresh fruit

Cottage cheese with sweetcorn

Tomato salsa dip

Go Greek

For an all-Greek lunchbox, try pitta fingers with houmous and **taramasalata** dips, plus a tub of Greek salad. To make a Greek salad, mix slices of tomato (or a handful of cherry tomatoes) with cubes of cucumber and rings of red onion. Sprinkle some black olives and a few cubes of feta cheese over the top, and then drizzle on a lemon and olive oil dressing. Mix up and munch!

Bored with bread?

Can't face another sandwich this week? Fancy a change?
Get your carbohydrate with a tub of rice or pasta.

It's not bread, but...

If you don't want to eat bread, rice and pasta are tasty alternatives. Both contain fibre and carbohydrates, so can contribute towards a balanced diet. Another good thing about rice and pasta? Whatever you can put in a sandwich, you can probably add to a tub of pasta or rice!

CHECK IT OUT!

If you have a wheat **allergy**, check the label on packets of pasta to make sure you are choosing a wheat-free variety.

Great grain

Rice is a grain and, like wheat for bread, it can be milled in two ways. White rice has the bran taken out. Brown rice still has the bran and tastes nutty. It has lots more fibre and lots of vitamin B.

Nice rice

Rice is quick and easy to cook and tastes great cold as well as hot. If you cook some rice the night before, keep leftovers in the fridge and add some vegetables the next day. Try adding sweetcorn, chopped green and red peppers, cucumber, onion and chopped tomato. Alternatively, try some chopped chicken or some tuna for a protein punch. For extra taste, sprinkle with a little soy sauce – but not too much as it is very salty.

Bite size

There are many different sorts of rice: basmati, long grain, short grain, fragrant Thai rice and Japanese sticky rice to name a few. There is even such a thing as wild rice, which is black!

Wild rice

Pasta facta

Like bread, pasta can also be made with both white or brown flour. Pasta cooks quickly, is sold in all shapes and sizes, and can be mixed with just about anything. For a really fun lunch, mix a whole load of different pasta shapes together, add your favourite cooked, chopped vegetables and a couple of spoonfuls of meat or fish. Tasty!

Try it!

Enjoy fried rice? Boiled or steamed rice tastes just as nice and is better for you.

21

A world of bread

Most countries and cultures have their own types of bread. Here are just a few to get your teeth into...

Flatbreads

Many countries use flour and water to make their bread, but not yeast. This means that their bread doesn't rise so they have flat bread, like pancakes. In Mexico, they have tortillas, in India they eat chapattis and paratha, and in Greece, they make pitta breads.

Chapatti

Fancy a fajita?

Ready-cooked flatbreads, such as tortillas, are available in packs from shops and supermarkets. For a lunchbox special, wrap a tortilla around your favourite sandwich filling. Filled tortillas are called fajitas. Remember to tuck in one end or the filling will end up in your lap instead of your mouth!

Fajita wrap

Weblink

Find out more about different Mexican breads by visiting www.elbalero.gob.mx/kids/about/html/did/bread.html

Special breads

In many cultures, certain foods are prepared for special occasions. Cholla is a bread eaten by Jewish families to celebrate the **Sabbath**. It is a plaited loaf made with eggs and butter and sprinkled with sesame and poppy seeds.

Bread for the dead

In Mexico, the Day of the Dead is a time to remember and celebrate those who have died. There are street parades and special sweets and foods. People make a bread called 'pan de los muertos', which means 'bread of the dead'. It is shaped like a skull or decorated with bones made from bread. Bakers hide a small plastic skeleton in each loaf. The person who bites into it will have good luck.

Heavy bread

Stollen is the name of a sweet, cake-like loaf made in Germany. It is a delicious mixture of dried fruit, **candied** cherries, marzipan and cinnamon. It is so full of lovely things that it is very heavy to carry!

Bread – the sweet treat

You never know, the school canteen may surprise you one day and give you a choice of delicious puddings made with bread.

Cream with your bread?

Call this bread? Looks more like pudding to me! Bread is so versatile that it is used in many sweet dishes, too. Bread-and-butter pudding is made from layers of sliced bread and butter with eggs, currants, milk and cream.

Summer slices

For a yummy and healthy summer pudding try... summer pudding! This delicious pudding is made by lining a bowl with slices of white bread and then filling it with a mixture of berries, such as redcurrants, strawberries, blackcurrants and blueberries. It is chilled in the fridge overnight and then turned out onto a plate. The juice turns the bread red for a sensational summer surprise. Tasty, looks great and it's good for you!

Brown bread ice cream

Made with wholemeal breadcrumbs, this unusual ice cream is delicious. Eat it with some berries for a vitamin-packed pudding that's ultra yummy!

Bite size

In India, peshwari naan is a sweet flatbread filled with coconut, apples, almonds and sultanas.

Not so sweet!

Don't be fooled if you see the word 'sweetbreads'. Sweetbreads is the general name for the glands of animals such as pigs and cows, found near the heart and throat. Not quite what you might have been expecting!

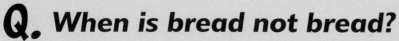

Peshwari naan

Q. **When is bread not bread?**
A. **When it's a breadfruit!**

A breadfruit is a large, green-skinned fruit that grows on trees in hot, tropical places such as the Caribbean. Although it is called a fruit, it is cooked like a potato – mashed, roasted or turned into chips!

Pinboard

Check out how bread is eaten in other countries.

India

Paratha and puri are fried Indian breads that are used to scoop up food. Puri is eaten as a starter in Indian restaurants and is usually served with curry piled on top – yum!

United States

Americans eat cornbread. It is made with cornmeal and is sometimes served with maple syrup.

Great Britain

This special loaf is made to celebrate the Christian Harvest Festival. The loaf looks like a bundle of wheat and sometimes has a little dough mouse running up it.

China

In China, deep-fried dough sticks are eaten for breakfast or as a snack.

Italy

In Italy, ciabatta bread is toasted and topped with tomatoes for a light snack. This is called bruschetta.

France

The French enjoy croissants and brioche for breakfast.

Quiz time

Multiple-choice

1. Which of the foods below provide carbohydrate as a sugar?

a. naan bread
b. chocolate cake
c. biscuits
d. bagels

2. Which of the following is not a type of bread?

a. ciabatta
b. fruit loaf
c. fibre
d. rye

3. Which of these fillings makes a healthy sandwich?

a. turkey with tomato
b. ham and cheese
c. tuna and celery
d. all of the above

4. Which of the following steps is not part of making bread?

a. mixing the dough
b. baking the bread
c. slicing the bread
d. eating the bread

5. Which type of cake is healthiest?

a. carrot cake
b. fudge cake
c. cream cake
d. fried doughnut

Match the bread to its country

chapatti

Germany

Great Britain

pitta

Greece

stollen

tortilla

India

Mexico

ciabatta

Italy

harvest loaf

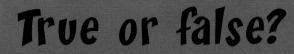

True or false?

1. Muesli bars are good for you.
2. Pitta fingers are good for dipping.
3. Greek salad contains feta cheese.
4. Fibre is bad for you.
5. Basmati rice is black.
6. Pasta takes two days to cook.
7. Mexicans like to eat cholla bread.
8. A fajita is a filled tortilla.
9. Stollen contains candied cherries.
10. Breadfruit is a type of bread.

What's the answer?

1. What could you eat as an alternative to bread?
2. Why is bread an important part of a balanced diet?
3. Can you think of three fantastic fajita fillings?
4. What is fibre?
5. Plan a lunchbox menu for a week so that every day you eat a different type of bread?

Answers

True or false?
1. TRUE
2. TRUE
3. TRUE
4. FALSE
5. FALSE
6. FALSE
7. FALSE
8. TRUE
9. TRUE
10. FALSE

Multiple choice
1. b and c – chocolate cake and biscuits
2. c – fibre
3. d – all of the above
4. d – eating the bread
5. a – carrot cake

Match the bread with its country
pitta – Greece
chapatti – India
tortilla – Mexico
stollen – Germany
ciabatta – Italy
harvest loaf – Great Britain

What's the answer?
There is not necessarily a right or a wrong answer to these questions, so discuss your answers with your teacher or a parent.

Glossary

allergy This is when you have a bad reaction, such as a rash or difficulty breathing, when you've eaten a certain type of food

candied Fruit such as cherries, orange peel and lemon peel which have been cooked, chopped and mixed with sugar and syrup to create very sweet, tiny pieces of fruit

carbohydrate This is the part of the food that you eat that gives your body energy

dough A thick mixture of flour and water that is used to make bread and pizza bases

fibre This is the part of your food that helps your digestion work properly and makes sure you go to the toilet regularly

grains These are the parts of plants which are grown as food, such as wheat and rice

houmous Mashed, cooked chickpeas mixed with oil to make a dip or spread

kneaded Mixing together the separate ingredients of bread to make dough

minerals Substances found in foods we eat that keep our bodies healthy, such as calcium which helps strengthen bones and teeth

muesli This is a mix of grains, nuts and chopped fruit that is usually eaten for breakfast

nutrients Substances such as vitamins and minerals that are found in the food we eat

portion A helping of one type of food to be eaten at one meal

processed When a food has been through a series of actions to make it look different from its natural state

protein Part of the food that we eat that helps us to grow muscles and keeps us healthy

proving This is also known as rising and is when bread dough with added yeast is left somewhere warm to rise before it is baked

Sabbath The Sabbath is known as the Lord's Day in the Jewish religion and is celebrated each Saturday

Taramasalata A dip or spread made from crushed fish eggs mixed with yoghurt

vitamins Substances found in food that are essential to keep us healthy. There are many different vitamins, such as A and C

wholegrain The whole of the wheat grain

yeast Yeast is a substance added to bread dough to make it rise. Flat bread does not have any yeast in it

Index

Parents' and teachers' notes

- Ask the children about bread. Do they eat a lot of it? What sort of bread do they eat? When and how do they eat it? Do they think bread is good for them?

- Discuss what the children eat for lunch and whether or not their meals involve bread. If they have a packed lunch, do they have sandwiches? If they have school lunches, is bread available? Discuss with the children if they think they eat healthy lunches. If not, how could their lunches be improved?

- When you've read the book, look back at the 'Lunch choices'. What do the children think about these? Have they tried them already? Would they like to try them? Ask the children to think about making their own lunchboxes using bread. What would they have?

- Were the children surprised by anything in the book? For example, did they think of bread as being sweet as well as savoury?

- Build a 'Yum' and a 'Yuk' sandwich. Ask the children to cut out pictures of their favourite sandwich fillings and the most disgusting ones they can think of. Build a fun montage of the fillings on the wall.

- If you can, organize a bread tasting. Ask the children to bring in as many different types of bread as possible. Divide into small bite-size pieces and encourage the children to try each one. Ask the children to write down words to describe each bread and to mark it out of ten for flavour and texture. For any tastings, ask each child to bring in a letter from their parents or guardians granting permission.